Wilderr

Classroom Questions

A SCENE BY SCENE TEACHING GUIDE

Amy Farrell

SCENE BY SCENE
ENNISKERRY, IRELAND

Scene by Scene
Enniskerry
Wicklow, Ireland.
www.scenebysceneguides.com

Wilderness Classroom Questions by Amy Farrell. —1st ed.
ISBN 978-1-910949-52-8

Contents

The Eyes

Summary

Brothers Johnny and Tom stand in the snow, looking into a pen of dogs. Most of the dogs howl, but one with striking eyes stares at them. The dog's eyes are an indescribable colour, close to blue or turquoise.

The boys back away from the dog and bump into a huge man who asks why they are there.

Questions

1.   What makes it difficult for the boys to name the colour of the dog's eyes?

2.   What are the other dogs doing?

3.   What is the dog with the unusual eyes doing?

4.   Describe this dog's eyes.

5.   Describe the man the brothers back into.

Chapter 1

Summary

Johnny and Tom's mother, Sandra, booked an adventure holiday for the three of them to Finland.

Their father, Frank, was previously married to a woman called Rosemary. She is the mother of Gráinne, Frank's daughter.

Frank and Rosemary's relationship broke down and they argued a lot. One night, after their rude neighbour called the Guards about the noise, they decided they couldn't live together anymore.

When Rosemary left, Frank told Gráinne that her mother was on holiday. Frank heard she had gone to New York. Rosemary phoned her parents a few times a year and sent her love to Gráinne, but that was all. She did not contact Gráinne.

For a long time it was just Frank and Gráinne and although they were lonely, they were together.

Then Frank met Sandra at a concert and she moved in shortly afterwards. The three of them were happy together.

Sandra and Frank told Gráinne that Sandra was pregnant. Gráinne loved Johnny, the new baby, and although life changed, she felt looked after.

When Tom was born, Johnny was very jealous and demanding, but Frank always made time for Gráinne.

Gráinne became more difficult as a teenager, she was unhappy and unfriendly. Frank and Sandra knew it was a phase, but Frank found it hard, sometimes blaming himself and feeling guilty, at other times thinking Gráinne was selfish, like her mother.

Gráinne was caught mitching from school and was suspended. She was also caught shoplifting. She left school two months before the Leaving Cert exams.

When Gráinne threw a cup at Sandra, Frank suggested that Sandra take a break with the boys, but Sandra refused.

Frank hears that Rosemary, Gráinne's mother, is coming home. This changes Sandra's mind about taking a break and she tells the boys about the trip to Finland.

Questions

1. What background details do you learn about Johnny and Tom as this chapter begins?

2. What were the boys doing when their mother came home from work?

3. What does their mother do when she gets in?
   What does this tell you about her personality?

4. What announcement does their mother have for them?

5. How do the boys react to their mother's news?

6. Why is their school principal happy to let the boys go?

7. What reason does Sandra give for the boys' father and Gráinne, their sister, staying at home?

8. Why does Frank, their father, play loud music as he turns into the drive?
   What does the backstory here reveal about his character?

9. What are your first impressions of Mrs Newman?

10. What happened Frank and Rosemary's relationship?

11. What made them argue about Gráinne's education?
    Does this sound like a reasonable argument to you?

12. Why did the Guards call to Frank and Rosemary's door?
    How does this make them feel?

13. How does Frank know that Mrs Newman phoned the Guards?

14. What did Frank and Rosemary agree that night?
    What is your response to this?

15. Whose idea was the trip to Finland?

16. Describe what happened when Rosemary left Frank.

17. How did Frank explain Rosemary's absence to Gráinne?
    Is this fair?
    Why did he say this?
    What is your reaction to this?

18. Where did Rosemary go?

19. Does Rosemary have a lot of contact with Gráinne?
    What is your reaction to this?

20. What was life like, when it was just Frank and Gráinne?

21. How did Frank meet Sandra?
    Did they get on well?

22. Did Sandra and Gráinne get on well in the beginning?
    Give examples to support your answer.

23. How did Frank explain Sandra moving in to Gráinne?
    Is he honest with his daughter?
    Does he strike you as a good parent? Explain your view.

24. What is life like with Sandra living wih Frank and
    Gráinne?
    Have things improved for them?

25. How did Gráinne react to the news of Sandra's pregnancy?
    Does her reaction surprise you?

26. How does Gráinne feel about the new baby?

27. What is life like once Johnny is born?
    Does Gráinne feel left out?

28. How were things different when Tom was born?

29. How did Johnny react to his new brother?
    Is this unusual?

30. Did Frank make time for Gráinne, after Tom's arrival?
    Give examples in your answer.

31. From what we have read so far, what sort of man is
    Frank?

32. How did Gráinne change when she became a teenager?
    Is this unusual?

33. How did Frank feel about the change in his daughter?

34. How did Gráinne react to Frank's invitation to the Bad Ass?
What is significant about this restaurant in particular?

35. As a teenager, how did Gráinne treat Sandra?
What is your reaction to this?

36. Why did Frank keep his distance from Gráinne at this stage?

37. What different things did Gráinne do that got her into trouble?
What is your reaction to her actions here?

38. Why did it matter that Gráinne left school?
Comment on her timing here.

39. What made Frank suggest that Sandra and the boys needed a break?
What is your response to Gráinne's behaviour here?

40. What was the sweetest thing Sandra had seen in a long time?
How did Gráinne respond to Sandra seeing her?

41. What news do they receive about Rosemary, Gráinne's mother?

42. How does Sandra react to this news?
Do you understand how she is feeling?
How would you feel, in her position?

43.   On the basis of this chapter, what are your impressions of Frank, Sandra and Gráinne?

44.   How do you feel about Rosemary's return?

The Bedroom

Summary

Gráinne is curled up on her bed.

She knows that Frank and Sandra are talking about her.

She thinks they hate her.

She hates them.

Questions

1. What insight into how Gráinne is thinking and feeling does this section give you?

Chapter 2

Summary

Sandra, Johnny and Tom go to get thermal underclothes, gloves, socks and scarves.

When Gráinne threw the cup at Sandra, the boys heard it hit the wall. They knew that something was definitely wrong.

Gráinne tells the boys that her mother is going to come and take her away and they are glad to hear it.

Johnny and Tom are a bit sad that their father is not going on the trip, but they are still happy to be going with their mother at the same time.

The journey to Helsinki requires three flights. A man from Winter Safaris is waiting for them at the airport.

They go to their hotel and the boys dress for the cold and go out to play. Just as they start throwing snowballs, they hear a howl.

Questions

1. What different things do Sandra, Johnny and Tom have to get for the trip?
   What does this tell you about the weather conditions they are expecting?

2. What extra items do Johnny and Tom want to get?

3. How did Johnny and Tom react when they heard the cup hitting the wall?
   How would you have reacted, in their position?

4. How did Johnny and Tom know that something was definitely wrong?

5. How do the boys react when Gráinne says her mother is going to take her away?
   Do you understand why they feel this way?
   What does their reaction here tell you about their relationship with Gráinne?

6. Are the boys upset that Frank is not going on holiday with them?

7. What is different about Sandra's behaviour when Frank is not around?

8. Describe the journey to Helsinki.

9. Do the boys get on well? Include examples in your answer.

10. What do the boys see out the plane window as they land?

How do the boys react to this sight?

How would you feel, in their position?

11. How long is this holiday for?

12. What details do you notice about the landscape?

13. Describe their hotel.

14. What does Sandra say they will do first?

How do the boys respond?

What would you do first, if you were there?

15. What do the brothers want to buy at hotel reception?

Are you surprised that they are not allowed to buy this item?

16. Why does Tom hit Johnny as they lean across the counter?

Do you understand why he does this?

How does Sandra react?

17. Describe their hotel room.

Are they happy with it?

Would you be happy with it?

18. Where do the boys go?

19. What do they hear when they go outside?

How does this change the atmosphere?

20.   Do you think they will enjoy this holiday? Support your answer with references to the story.

The Bus

Summary

Gráinne gets the bus to the airport to meet her mother.

She is alone.

She carries a photograph, but tells herself that she would know her mother without it.

Questions

1. Where is Gráinne going?

2. Why does she want to do this alone, do you think?

3. It says that the speed of the bus made Gráinne's hand shake.
   Is there any other reason why her hand might be shaking?

4. Why does she have a photograph?

5. Why does she tell herself she won't need the photograph?

6. Do you feel sorry for Gráinne here?

7. What is the atmosphere like at this point?

8. How would you feel, in Gráinne's position?

Chapter 3

Summary

The boys realise that they are hearing the howls of more than one dog. They walk towards a high wire fence and see a lane. In this lane they discover a row of snowmobiles under the trees and beyond that, a village of dog kennels.

The dogs are chained up and quite friendly. Tom has never seen so much poo before. He feels the heat of the dogs as he walks among them, looking at the amazing colours of their eyes.

One dog blocks their way and the boys can tell he is the pack leader by the way he holds himself. The boys find it impossible to name this dog's eye colour, it is something close to blue or turquoise. Its eyes are human-like, Tom suggests it is as if a person is trapped in the dog.

Keeping their eyes on the dog, they back into an enormous man. He tells the boys they should not be there.

The dogs are glad to see the man. He gets the boys to help him change the straw in the dogs' kennels.

The first thing Sandra notices when the boys return an hour later is the smell. They tell her about the dogs and helping the man. They do not tell her that Tom bought a knife.

Questions

1. How do the boys know that there is more than one dog?

2. Describe the fence.

3. How does Johnny walk on the ice?

4. Why does Tom move closer to his brother?

5. What sort of night is it?

6. What do the boys discover?

7. How do the dogs react when they see the boys?

8. Do you already know anything about huskies? Give as much detail as you can.

9. Why does Tom walk carefully among the dogs?

10. What do the boys notice about the dogs' eyes?

11. What is special about the dog that makes them stop? What is special about this dog's eyes?

12. Describe the man the boys back into. Is he pleased to find them here?

13. The book began with this section. Why is it included twice, do you think?

14. How do the dogs respond to the man?

15.   What do the boys notice on the man's belt?

       What is your reaction to this?

16.   What does the dog do to Johnny?

17.   What do the boys help the man with?

       Is it a hard job?

       Would you help him, in their position?

18.   What is the first thing Sandra notices when the boys come back?

       What does this tell you?

19.   How does Sandra know that the boys are frozen?

20.   Why don't they know the man's name?

21.   What do the boys talk to Sandra about?

       Are they excited about the next day, do you think?

22.   What do they hide from Sandra?

       What is your reaction to this?

       Why do they keep this from her?

The Airport (1)

Summary

Rosemary's plane is delayed. Gráinne feels that she has spent most of her life waiting. She does not recognise any of the other people that are waiting there.

The screen changes to show the word 'LANDED'. Gráinne checks the photograph again.

Questions

1. Why is Gráinne still waiting in the airport?

   Is it significant that she does not recognise anyone else who is waiting?

   Does this surprise you?

2. Why does Gráinne feel she has spent her life waiting?

   Do you feel sorry for her?

   How must she be feeling, as she waits?

3. Describe the atmosphere at this point.

4. Why does she look at the photograph again?

Chapter 4

Summary

The boys' excitement wakes them up and they go down to the dining room without waiting for Sandra.

The dining room is very quiet and they notice that there are no other children.

They quickly eat some chocolate cereal and get some cooked breakfast before Sandra comes down. She spots some chocolate on Johnny's lips.

Their guide, Aki, comes in and addresses the diners. They go outside and Sandra thinks about how glad she is to be there. She slips on the ice and is embarrassed.

The group get dressed in red padded suits and go to meet the huskies. Aki demonstrates how the sleds work.

The man from the night before, Kalle, arrives. He owns the dogs.

Kalle harnesses the dogs. Aki explains that the dogs follow Rock, the lead dog, and he follows Kalle, so reins and orders are not necessary.

Johnny and Tom want their own sleds, but Aki explains that they are too light to work the brake. Aki drives a snowmobile, not a dogsled.

The boys sit in Kalle's sled, in a narrow hollow. They begin to fight in the sled, but stop when Kalle leans over and speaks to them. He gives them a blanket and they set off. The boys are so excited that they shout.

Questions

1. What wakes the boys up the next morning?

2. What do the boys notice in the dining room?

3. What do the boys have for breakfast?

4. What do the boys call each other whenever they have a disagreement?
    Does this tell you anything about their relationship?

5. Why do the boys cover up what they had for breakfast?

6. Tom thinks that the no chocolate rule is stupid.
    Is this a stupid rule?
    What does it tell you about their mother, Sandra?

7. Describe the man that comes in to address the diners.

8. What are the sausages made from?

9. Sandra is glad to be away from the complications of home.
    What are these complications, as you see them?

10. How do the boys play in their suits?
    Does this sound like fun to you?

11. How do the huskies react as the people approach?

12. What makes Johnny think that Aki is good at his job?

13. What does Sandra think of the dogs' eyes?

14. How do the adults respond to the idea of travelling by dog sled?

15. Describe the dog sled.

16. What makes the sled stop and go?

17. Why are Johnny and Tom the only ones asking questions? Does this kind of thing happen much, in your experience?

18. Who is Kalle?

19. What makes the dogs go?

20. What is the lead dog's name?

21. What does Tom know by the dogs' tails?

22. How does Tom feel when Johnny calls him an eejit?

23. Why can't Johnny and Tom have their own sleds?

24. Why do the boys like Aki?

25. How does Aki travel?
    Why does he do this?

26. How will Johnny and Tom travel?

27. How does Kalle stop the boys fighting?

28. Why don't the boys want the blanket Kalle gives them?

29. What do the boys do when the dogs start running?

30.   Describe the mood at this point.

31.   Would you enjoy this sort of holiday? Give reasons for your answer.

The Airport (2)

Summary

Gráinne is looking at people meeting loved ones or waiting to be met. She is afraid that she has missed Rosemary.

As she scans the arrivals hall, a woman greets her. It is her mother. Gráinne feels nothing and wants to run away.

Her mother thanks her for meeting her. They decide to go for breakfast together.

Her mother tells Gráinne that she can call her Rosemary if she likes. Gráinne asks what she used to call her. Rosemary tries to hold herself together as she answers, "Mama".

Questions

1. Why is Gráinne scared?

2. Describe the people waiting to be met or recognised.
   Can you explain what they are doing and why they look this way?

3. How does Gráinne feel when she meets her mother?

4. Rosemary is glad that Gráinne met her.
   Would you have gone to the airport if you were Gráinne?
   Explain your reasons fully.

5. How is Rosemary feeling, do you think? Use examples from the text to support the points you make.

6. "She'd never heard this woman's voice before."
   How does this line make you feel?

7. What does Gráinne notice about Rosemary's accent?
   What does she think about this?

8. Why does Gráinne's mother tell her to call her Rosemary if she wants?

9. How does Rosemary react when Gráinne asks her what she used to call her?
   Why does she react like this?
   Do you feel sorry for Rosemary?

10. Describe the mood at this point.

Chapter 5

Summary

The dogs are working together to pull the sled at a fast pace. They go over a hill and into a forest. The boys think being in the sled is the best thing that has ever happened to them.

They head back into the forest as an empty sled pulls level with the boys. Kalle stops the team. The boys get out of the sled. Aki pulls up with their mother on the snowmobile.

She laughs with the boys about falling off. Kalle asks her what happened, but she does not know why she fell.

Johnny does not let Tom back in the sled, so Kalle lifts Johnny out to let Tom in before they set off again.

Questions

1.   What is travelling by sled like?

2.   Describe the way the dogs run.
        Why do they run like this?

3.   Are they travelling fast or slow?
        Find a quote to support your answer.

4.   Does the sled ride sound fun to you?

5.   Describe the landscape and surroundings.

6.   What do the boys hear as they are about to re-enter the
        forest?

7.   Why does Kalle stop the sled?

8.   Does Kalle have good control of the dogs?

9.   Who fell off their sled?
        Are they annoyed or embarrassed?
        How did it happen?

10.   Why can't Tom get back in the sled?
        How does Kalle fix the situation?

11.   What 'joke' does Kalle tell Tom?
        Do you think he is joking?

The Taxi

Summary

Gráinne waits in the taxi as her mother drops her bags off at Gráinne's Granny's.

The taxi driver asks Gráinne if Rosemary is her mother, but Gráinne does not answer.

Questions

1. What does Gráinne see out the taxi window?

2. Why doesn't Gráinne answer the taxi driver?

3. Which storyline interests you more? Give reasons for your answer.

Chapter 6

Summary

The boys are excited as they sled across a frozen lake. They feel cold as they enter a forest on the other side. The dogs stop when they reach a clearing where Aki waits.

Their mother asks them what they think of the sled ride. Tom says it is brilliant, but Johnny says it is boring, so Sandra chases him and shoves snow down his suit to make him change his mind.

Aki asks Tom to help him make the coffee. He hands him his big knife to split sticks. When Johnny sees this he wants a go, but Aki tells him he can do it the next time.

Aki arranges the coffee pot over the fire and the tired adults wait for it to be ready while the boys play in the snow.

Questions

1.   Where are they as the chapter begins?

2.   Does the landscape remind you of any other books, films or t.v. programmes? Give examples in your answer.

3.   Why is travelling over ice exciting?

4.   Where do they go, once they cross the ice?

5.   Describe the clearing where Aki waits.
Would you like to experience a place like this?
Does the setting here remind you of anywhere?

6.   What interesting thing does Aki do to the branch?

7.   How do the dogs relax, now that they have stopped?

8.   What does Sandra do to Johnny when he says travelling by sled is boring?
Why does she do this?
What does this demonstrate about Sandra's relationship with Johnny?

9.   What does Aki tell Tom about the Siberian Jay?

10.   How does Tom help Aki?
How does Johnny react to Tom helping?
What does Aki promise Johnny?
Is this fair?

11.   How are the group feeling, as they wait for their coffee?

12.   What do Johnny and Tom do to pass the time?

13.   Describe Johnny's and Tom's personalities, based on what we have read so far.

The Café

Summary

Gráinne feels a bit sick as she sits with her mother in a café. She feels like a kid, and is also very angry. She holds back though and does not let her anger take over.

When Rosemary invites her to talk about herself, Gráinne refuses, saying that it is like a crap film.

Rosemary begins to talk about herself and her life in New York. Gráinne asks her if she lives alone. Rosemary answers that she wanted to talk about other things first.

Rosemary says maybe she should not have come, that she thought it would be easy.

Gráinne says that she had always thought that nothing would matter when they saw each other again. This however, is clearly not the case. Gráinne tells Rosemary that she dislikes the way Rosemary talks and that she thinks she is dishonest.

Rosemary suggests that they start again, but Gráinne calls her suggestion crap, and leaves. Rosemary does not follow her.

Questions

1.   How does Gráinne feel, in the café with her mother?

2.   Why is Gráinne so angry?
Should Rosemary be expecting this?

3.   Why does Gráinne have to keep holding back with what she says?
How would you feel in her position?
How would you act towards Rosemary?
What would you say to her?

4.   How does Gráinne respond to her mother's invitation to tell her a bit about herself?
Do you understand Gráinne's reaction?
How does Rosemary respond?

5.   What different things does Gráinne find out about her mother during their conversation?

6.   What makes Rosemary say that maybe she should not have come?

7.   Are you surprised that Rosemary thought it would be easy to see Gráinne?

8.   What had Gráinne expected their meeting to be like?

9.   What makes Rosemary start to cry?

10. What does Gráinne tell Rosemary while she is crying?

    Is Gráinne being cruel or truthful here?

11. Why does Gráinne leave?

    Does she expect Rosemary to follow her, do you think?

    Do you think that Rosemary should follow her?

    Give reasons in your answer.

12. How is Gráinne feeling as the chapter ends?

    Do you expect her to meet Rosemary again? Explain your

    point of view.

Chapter 7

Summary

The boys are hungry and tired as they return to the hotel that night. When they stop, Kalle tells them to look after the dogs.

Tom loves looking after the dogs and does not feel tired at all. The boys delay going inside because they are enjoying being with the dogs, but Kalle tells them that the dogs must rest.

They work with Kalle for another hour and when everything is done, they go into the hotel.

Questions

1. Why are the boys so tired?

2. What funny thing do they see a dog do?

3. What is Tom hungry for?
    Why is this the case, do you think?

4. When they stop, what does Kalle tell the boys to do?

5. Why does Tom take off his gloves?

6. What do the dogs get for dinner?

7. How do the adults walk as they make their way to the hotel?
    Are they having a good time?

8. Why do the boys delay going inside?

9. Why does Kalle stop the boys from exciting the dogs?

10. Why are the dogs' bowls wooden?

11. Is caring for the dogs hard work?
    Does it sound like fun to you? Explain your answer.

12. Why does Johnny feel different as the chapter ends?

13. Have you ever been around working dogs?
    If so, what was it like?

The Bedroom

Summary

Gráinne sits on her bed, cutting up magazines. She feels that she does not belong anywhere.

The isolation she feels is different now. Previously, the future for her had meant her mother, Gráinne had imagined all that they would do together.

She thinks about all the things she likes about her father. She closes her eyes and when she opens them, he is in her room. He tells her he is sorry that things with her mother are not working out.

Frank says that Rosemary wants to call over, but Gráinne does not want to see her. Frank advises her to give Rosemary more time.

He tells Gráinne that he loves her.

She agrees to see her mother the following afternoon.

Frank says that the boys and Sandra are having a great time, but Gráinne does not care.

Questions

1. What is Gráinne doing?

2. Why does Gráinne's father always knock on her bedroom door before going in?
   Does this tell you anything about him?

3. Why does Gráinne feel like she does not belong?

4. What appeals to Gráinne about Punk music?

5. How does Gráinne know that she is home alone?

6. Does Gráinne like being at home on her own?

7. What has changed for Gráinne since meeting Rosemary?

8. How had she imagined life with her mother?
   What is your response to this?

9. What does Gráinne like about her father?
   What does this reveal about their relationship?

10. How does Gráinne treat her father?

11. What do they talk about?

12. What advice does Frank give Gráinne?
    Does this sound like good advice to you?

13. Are you surprised that Frank would like Rosemary to be happy? Explain your point of view.

14. Is Frank a good father? Explain your viewpoint, using examples.

15. Does Gráinne care about the boys and Sandra?

16. Is Gráinne a difficult daughter? Explain your point of view.

Chapter 8

Summary

The boys are sledding across the frozen lake, travelling north, where they will spend the night in a hut in the wilderness. It is snowing. They enter the forest.

They stop because the man from Belgium has fallen off his sled.

The dogs are not as fast as usual in the deep snow. It is difficult to see in the snow and the dark.

The boys suddenly fly out of the sled as it overturns, but they are unhurt.

They reach the hut and use the toilet before helping Kalle with the dogs.

When they go inside, they do not see their mother.

Questions

1.   How does Sandra wake Johnny up?

2.   What makes Johnny think that they are beginning the real safari?

3.   Describe the hut they will stay in, according to the brochure.

4.   What do the boys decide to get for Christmas?

5.   What makes the dogs slow down?

6.   Are the boys hurt when their sled topples over? Why did this happen, do you think?

7.   What makes Tom laugh?

8.   What does the hut look like? Does it sound inviting to you?

9.   "The giant will eat us if we don't hurry." Are the boys having a good time? Do the boys get on well together? Use examples from the text to support the points you make.

10.   How do the boys help Kalle? Does he appreciate their help?

The Kitchen (1)

Summary

Gráinne and Rosemary are in Gráinne's kitchen. Frank is somewhere in the house, he has stayed at home because Gráinne wants him to.

Gráinne realises how strange it must be for her father to see Rosemary. Gráinne tells Rosemary that she will give things with her a try.

Rosemary says that she wishes she could say something to make everything ok.

Rosemary begins explaining why she left. She tells Gráinne that she loves her and Gráinne feels like she will explode or die. She keeps calm though and listens to what her mother has to say.

Rosemary explains that she had to leave.

Gráinne feels different because she lets her mother speak, and chooses to listen.

Questions

1. Does Gráinne and Rosemary's conversation get off to a good start?

2. Gráinne no longer has friends.
   What does this tell you about Gráinne?

3. Why has Frank stayed home from work?
   Do you think it is difficult for Frank to see Rosemary?

4. What memory does Gráinne have about the garden?
   What is your response to this?

5. Does Rosemary really want to build a good relationship with Gráinne, in your opinion?
   What makes you say this?

6. Does Gráinne want to build a good relationship with her mother, in your opinion?
   What makes you say this?

7. How does Gráinne feel when Rosemary says that she loves her?
   Why, do you think, does she feel this way?

8. Does Gráinne find it difficult to listen to Rosemary?
   Should she hear her out and listen to her?
   What would you do, in her position?

9. How does Rosemary explain why she left?

10. Why does Gráinne listen to her?

11. Has their conversation gone well? Give reasons for your answer.

12. Do you feel sorry for Gráinne?

13. Do you feel sorry for Rosemary?

Chapter 9

Summary

The boys cannot see their mother anywhere. Aki says she must have fallen. He and Kalle go out to look for her.

The boys are concerned, but reassured by how calm Aki and Kalle are. The other adults are sympathetic.

A woman working in the hut gives the boys hot chocolate.

Johnny realises that if their mother had fallen off her sled, her dogs would have arrived alone. Her team of dogs did not catch up with Kalle though. The boys suspect that Hastro, the tricky dog in her team, might be to blame.

Kalle and Aki return without Sandra. Aki says he will phone the rescue people.

The snow falls thick and fast.

Aki and Kalle look at the map. Aki checks the first aid box.

Tom and Johnny slip out and take Kalle's dogs and a pair of sleds, hitching two to each sled. Johnny takes Rock.

Tom feels disloyal about what they are doing, but he is certain that it is the right thing to do.

Johnny leads the way. Aki and Kalle run over the snow and call out, but the boys keep going.

They travel through the cold and dark, sure that the huskies will help them to find their mother.

Questions

1. "Their mother wasn't there."
    How do you feel when you read this line?

2. What does Aki think has happened to their mother?
    How does Tom react to this?
    How does Johnny react to this?

3. Do Aki and Kalle seem worried?
    Are the boys very worried?

4. How do the other adults treat the boys?

5. Why don't the boys take their suits off?

6. Describe the woman that works in the hut.

7. What is cooking for dinner?
    Is Tom happy about this?
    Would you be happy about this?

8. What does Johnny realise about their mother's dogs and
    sled?

9. What do the boys think might have happened?

10. What does Aki say must have happened?

11. When they return without Sandra, what does Aki plan to
    do next?

12. Describe the snowfall at this point.
    Why is this significant?

13. How is Tom feeling now?

14. Why, do you think, do Kalle and Aki look at the map?

15. Why does Aki check the first aid box?

16. Describe the atmosphere at his point.

17. Where do Johnny and Tom go?
    What do they do?
    Is this a foolish idea?
    How will Johnny make Rock go?

18. How does Tom feel about what they are doing?
    What would you do, in his position?

19. Why did nobody stop Johnny and Tom?

20. Does Tom find it difficult to manage the sled?

21. How does Johnny navigate the sled?

22. Is Johnny confident that they will find Sandra?

23. Describe the scene as the chapter ends.

24. What makes this a tense moment?

25. What will happen next, in your opinion?

The Kitchen (2)

Summary

Gráinne is at the kitchen window. Rosemary is out in the garden, looking at the plants she planted there years ago.

Rosemary has been gone a long time and Gráinne begins to lose the good feeling from earlier as her anger returns.

As Rosemary comes back in, Gráinne tries to stop her anger.

Questions

1.   Where is Gráinne?

2.   What is Rosemary doing?

3.   What makes Gráinne sit down?
     Why is she so self-conscious, do you think?

4.   How does Gráinne start feeling as she waits for her
     mother? Explain this change in her.

5.   How is she feeling when Rosemary comes back in?

6.   How do the cold and dark add to the atmosphere here?

7.   Is Gráinne a very angry person, in your view?

Chapter 10

Summary

Johnny and Tom continue through the trees, with the light of the snowmobile behind them.

Tom feels that there is no need to worry as Rock knows what he is doing.

Johnny is not worried about getting caught, as it will mean more people to help find their mother.

A branch hits Tom's cheek and he thinks he feels blood. He is not really scared though.

Tom feels that Aki and Kalle let him down. He thinks they should have been faster and more worried about Sandra. He feels that they downplayed things and treated him and Johnny like kids.

A branch hits Johnny across the side of his face, hurting him badly.

Johnny recognises where they are as the spot where they fell out of the sled earlier. He stops and talks to Tom.

They should have passed Sandra already. Johnny thinks that Sandra didn't fall off at all. He reckons that Hastro ran off with their mother on the sled.

They do not wait for the adults, guessing that they would stop searching to bring the boys back to the hut. They decide to get going, planning to follow the dogs.

The falling snow helps numb Johnny's face.

Tom is feeling horrible, wishing he had never come, when his sled gets stuck. He hears a dog bark somewhere.

Johnny struggles to push his own sled clear.

Tom strains to push his sled forward. A branch catches his hat. When he grabs it, he loses hold of his sled.

Tom struggles to fight his way clear of a branch, back to Johnny.

They start moving again, shouting 'wilderness' as they go, so that their mother can hear them.

They think they hear her in the distance.

Questions

1.   Why can Tom see Johnny now?

2.   Is Tom worried about where Rock is leading them?
   Does this make sense to you?

3.   Why isn't Johnny worried about Aki catching up with them?

4.   Why does Tom shout, "Are we there yet?"
   Is he taking this seriously?

5.   Is Tom frightened?

6.   How does Tom hurt his face?

7.   Why does Tom feel let down by Aki and Kalle?
   Is he entitled to feel this way, do you think?

8.   How does Johnny get injured?
   Is it serious?

9.   Where do they stop?
   What should have happened by now?
   What does Johnny think has happened to Sandra?

10.   What makes the boys decide not to wait for Aki and Kalle?
    Is this a good choice, do you think?
    What would you do here, in their position?

11.   How is Johnny feeling physically at this point?

12.   How does the snow help Johnny?

13.   Are the brothers brave, do you think?

14.   Why doesn't Johnny like being amongst thick trees again?

15.   What happens Tom's sled?

16.   What does Tom hear?

17.   Is it easy to get the sleds moving again?
           Are the boys in difficulty here?

18.   What happens when Tom grabs his hat?
           Are you concerned about what might happen next?

19.   Why do the boys keep shouting "Wil-derness!!" as they go?
           Is this a good strategy?

20.   What do the boys hear as the chapter ends?

21.   How do you view the boys' attempts to find their mother?
           Is what they are doing daring or dangerous?

22.   What state must Sandra be in, do you think?

23.   Does this search and rescue attempt remind you of any other books or films that you have come across? Explain your answer.

The Kitchen (3)

Summary

Gráinne feels like a fight is taking place inside her ribcage, but she tells Rosemary she is fine. Gráinne feels a bit better controlling herself.

Rosemary talks about when she left. She does not regret going, but she does regret not being with Gráinne.

Rosemary cries a lot before going on. Gráinne wants to know why Rosemary did not visit. Rosemary says it was because of guilt. Rosemary thought that Gráinne and Frank were better off without her.

Gráinne thought that Rosemary left because of her. Rosemary tells her that it was nothing like that.

Gráinne asks why Rosemary decided to come and see her now. Rosemary explains that her best friend, Bernie, died. This made her realise that she had made a terrible mistake, so she came to see Gráinne.

Questions

1. How is Gráinne feeling as this section begins?

2. What hurtful, truthful thing does Rosemary tell Gráinne about leaving her and Frank?
    What is your response to this?

3. What does Rosemary regret?
    What is your response to this?

4. How does Rosemary cry?
    What makes her cry like this, do you think?

5. What reason does Rosemary give for never visiting?
    Is this excuse good enough in your view?

6. What made Rosemary go so far away?

7. What did Gráinne think Rosemary's reason for leaving was?
    What is your response to this?

8. Why has Rosemary come to see Gráinne *now*?

9. "Gráinne didn't have a friend like that. She didn't really have friends at all."
    What insight does this give you into Gráinne's life?
    How does this make you feel?
    Can you explain why Gráinne lacks friends?

10. Does Rosemary's reason for coming to see Gráinne make sense to you?

Do you think it is possible for them to build a relationship? Explain your view.

Chapter 11

Summary

The boys have only heard their mother's voice once, but they keep looking for her. They keep calling out, confident that the dogs will find her.

They hear her again and realise that the dogs are leading them to her.

They travel down a slope and find their mother next to a boulder, her sled broken, the team's straps tangled in the branches of a log.

Sandra thinks she has broken her leg. She tells her sons that they are great.

Rock stands over Hastro and holds his neck with his teeth. Hastro crawls out from under him.

Sandra shivers uncontrollably. Tom realises they need a fire to warm her. They clear a space in the snow and start gathering wood.

Johnny knows they cannot let Sandra fall asleep and keeps her talking.

She says she was behind everyone else when Hastro swerved off the path.

Tom uses his knife to slice the wood. Sandra tells him he should have told her about the knife, but Johnny says Tom was right because otherwise they would be stuck now.

Johnny keeps her talking, asking her what happened next. She says at first she thought Hastro had taken a shortcut, that it did not seem that long until she reached the point where they have found her.

Tom realises they have nothing to light the wood and feels really annoyed, but calms down when Johnny has an idea.

Tom uses their mother's lighter to get the fire going. They put snow on Sandra's neck and forehead to try to revive her.

The boys make a bed of pine needles close to the fire and untangle the dogs. Tom snuggles up to his mother and Johnny sits close by.

She tells them that her sled hit something and she broke her leg. They tell her all about the hut and their journey to find her.

Johnny realises he lost Kalle's hat, so Rock has managed to find Sandra on his own.

Sandra tells the boys she loves them. They ask if they can get a husky for Christmas and she agrees.

They spend the night sleeping and tending to the fire. Johnny wakes to see that the dogs have surrounded them, a moment he shares with his mother.

Questions

1. Do the boys manage to locate Sandra?

2. Why don't the boys need to direct the dogs?

3. Describe the scene when the boys find their mother.

4. What scares Tom and Johnny when they reach her?

5. What injury has their mother sustained?

6. How do you feel as the boys kneel beside Sandra?

7. What does Rock do to Hastro?
   Why does he do this?

8. What state is Sandra in?

9. What does Tom realise they need?
   Is this clever of him?

10. What happened, according to Sandra?

11. How do they light the fire?

12. Do Tom and Johnny make a good team? Use examples to support your answer.
    Has their relationship changed since they arrived in the wilderness?

13. How do the boys revive their mother?

14.   What do they do with the dogs?

15.   What makes Tom feel so happy?

16.   Why does Tom feel like a different boy?

17.   How does Sandra respond to hearing about the boys' adventure finding her?

18.   What does Johnny realise about Kalle's hat?
             What does this mean?

19.   How do they spend the night?

20.   What do the dogs do during the night?
             Why do they do this?

21.   What is the mood like as the chapter ends?

The Door

Summary

Gráinne and Rosemary have made plans to meet again, but Gráinne has turned down Rosemary's offer of going to live with her in New York.

Rosemary is about to leave as Frank comes downstairs and answers the phone.

Rosemary leaves and Gráinne goes to talk to Frank. He tells her that Sandra and the boys are missing.

Questions

1. What plans have Gráinne and Rosemary made?

2. Are you surprised that Gráinne turned down Rosemary's offer of living with her in New York?

3. What is the mood like in this chapter?

4. When Rosemary leaves, Gráinne waits to talk to her dad. Does her wish to talk to Frank surprise you?

5. Are you concerned when Frank says Sandra and the boys are missing? Explain your response.

Chapter 12

Summary

The boys wake up freezing, covered in snow. They cannot wake Sandra. They rub her face and shoulders to rouse her.

Sandra moans and shivers.

Tom starts to gather more firewood while Johnny rekindles a tiny flame. They slowly feed the fire, but then the tepee of branches protecting it collapses and Tom has to struggle with it again.

Johnny rubs their mother's face while Tom lights the fire, burning his thumb in the process.

Johnny tries to move their mother so that she faces the heat. Despite the fire, Sandra is unresponsive. Tom begins to cry.

Sandra's eyes open, she asks Tom what is wrong. He tells her he is fine and they watch the fire.

Aki, Kalle and the rescue team find them by the fire. They will airlift Sandra to hospital once they reach the lake.

Aki tells the brothers that Sandra would have died without them, that they have saved her life.

Tom falls asleep in the sled. Johnny does not shout "wilderness", as he does not want to wake him.

Questions

1. What state are the boys in when they wake up?

2. Why are they so concerned when Sandra does not wake? How do you feel, reading this part?

3. How do they rouse their mother?

4. What noises are the dogs making? Why do they behave this way?

5. What condition is Sandra in? What is your reaction to this?

6. What does Tom do next?

7. What stops Johnny from running towards the sound of the engine?

8. How does Johnny get the fire going again?

9. Are you impressed by the boys here?

10. Why does the fire pose such a problem for them?

11. Can you explain Sandra's condition at this point?

12. How do you feel when Sandra opens her eyes and looks at Tom?

13. What makes this section so tense?

14.   Describe the rescue team.

15.   Why does Aki salute the boys?
        What is your response to hearing him say this?

16.   How did Kalle find them?

17.   What stops Johnny from shouting "wilderness" in the
        sled?
        Does this tell you anything about his relationship with his
        brother?

The Airport (3)

Summary

Gráinne waits with an impatient, anxious Frank in the airport. She is surprised by how happy she is to see Johnny and Tom. Tom has got a toy husky as a present for her.

Sandra is in a wheelchair, her leg is broken in two places.

Sandra and Gráinne smile at one another.

Tom tells Gráinne that they are getting a husky for Christmas.

Questions

1. How do you know Frank is anxious as he waits in the airport?

2. How does Gráinne feel when she sees the boys?

3. What did Tom get Gráinne?

4. Are Sandra and the boys glad to be home, do you think?

5. Why does Frank laugh at the end?

6. Are they a happy family as the story ends? Explain your answer.

Further Questions

1. What did you like about this novel?
    Give examples in your answer.

2. What did you dislike about this novel?
    Give examples in your answer.

3. Who is your favourite character?
    What do you like or admire about them?

4. Which character do you dislike most? Explain what
    makes you dislike them.

5. What different elements of the story combine to make
    this novel exciting?

6. Does this story have a happy ending?
    Is it happy for all of the members of the family?

7. Was there anything in the story that you would have
    liked to know more about? Explain your answer,
    using examples.

8. Would this story make a good movie?
    What actors would you choose to play the lead roles?
    Explain your choices.

9. Would you like to go on an adventure holiday like the one in this novel? Why/why not?
   What would be your ideal adventure holiday?

10. Did this novel teach you anything about huskies?

11. Did this novel teach you anything about Finland?

12. Do the parents in this story have good relationships with their children? Include examples in your answer.

13. What does this story teach us about families?

14. What was your favourite section of the story?
    Why did this part appeal to you?

15. What was the saddest section of the story?
    What made it sad or moving?

16. Does this novel remind you of any other novels or films?
    Explain your view.

17. Would you recommend this novel to a friend?
    Why/ why not?

CLASSROOM QUESTIONS GUIDES

Books of questions, designed to save teachers time and lead
to rewarding classroom experiences.

www.SceneBySceneGuides.com

Lightning Source UK Ltd.
Milton Keynes UK
UKOW06f1803030616

275560UK00001B/26/P